FESTIVALS OF THE WORLD

FRANCE

 **Marshall Cavendish**
Benchmark
New York

This edition first published in 2011 in
the United States of America by
Marshall Cavendish Benchmark.

Marshall Cavendish Benchmark
99 White Plains Road
Tarrytown, NY 10591
Website: www.marshallcavendish.us

© Marshall Cavendish International (Asia)
Pte Ltd 2011
Originated and designed by Marshall Cavendish
International (Asia) Pte Ltd
A member of Times Publishing Limited
Times Centre, 1 New Industrial Road
Singapore 536196

Written by: Susan McKay
Edited by: Crystal Chan
Designed by: Lock Hong Liang/Steven Tan
Picture research: Thomas Khoo

Library of Congress Cataloging-in-Publication Data
McKay, Susan, 1972-
France / by Susan McKay.
p. cm. -- (Festivals of the world)
Includes bibliographical references and index.
Summary: "This book explores the exciting
culture and many festivals that are celebrated in
France"--Provided by publisher.
ISBN 978-1-60870-099-8
1. Festivals--France--Juvenile literature.
2. France--Social life and customs--
Juvenile literature. I. Title.
GT4849.A2M35 2011
944--dc22
2010000285
ISBN 978-1-60870-099-8

Printed in Malaysia

1 3 6 5 4 2

Contents

It's Festival Time . . .

The French are noted throughout the world for many things, including their style and food. Festivals are also a celebrated part of French culture. Delicious foods, terrific music, and amazing costumes are some of the wonders of a French *fête* [fette], or festival. Celtic dancing, a magnificent float parade, or a day with the Gypsies are all part of the excitement. Come along and join in the fun. It's festival time in France!

Where's France?

France is one of the oldest nations in Europe. It lies near the edge of the continent and has a long coastline on the Atlantic Ocean. There are many different land forms in France—mountains, forests, plains, and beaches. The capital, and the largest city, is Paris.

Who Are the French?

Thousands of years ago, a group of people known as the **Celts** lived in France. The Celts had a love of art and a great respect for nature. Many Celtic traditions are reflected in the customs and practices of the French, especially in the region of Brittany on the northwest coast.

Many years later, people from all over Europe traveled across the continent. When they reached France, they thought they had reached the edge of the world. At this time, the Americas had not been discovered yet. Many people settled in France and made it their home.

Today France is a mix of many different people from various ethnic backgrounds.

✳ A girl holding two baguettes [ba-GETZ], the delicious, crusty bread made famous by the French.

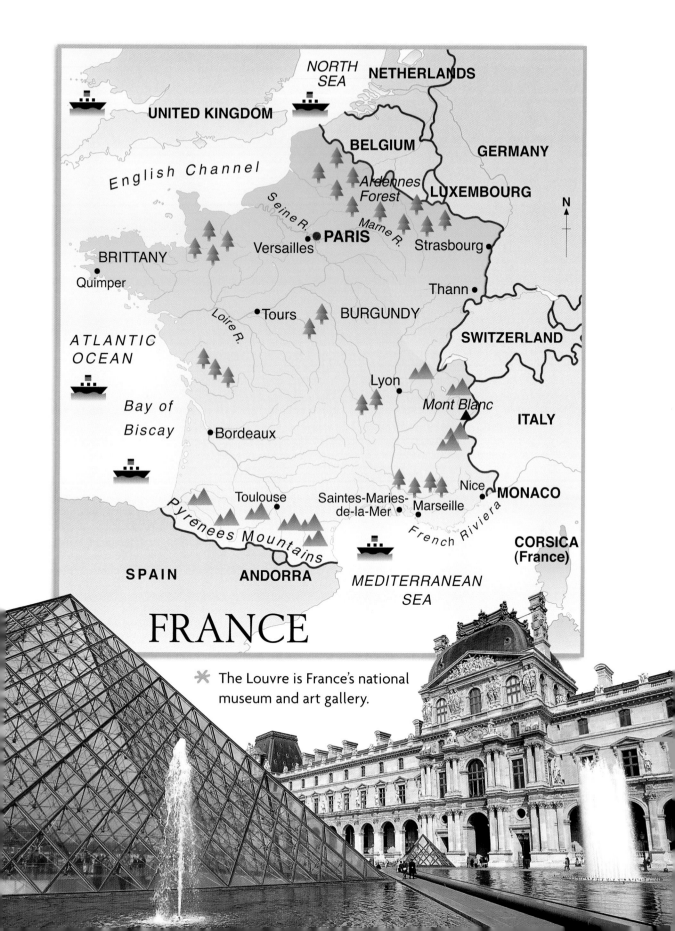

NORTH SEA

NETHERLANDS

UNITED KINGDOM

BELGIUM

GERMANY

English Channel

Ardennes Forest

LUXEMBOURG

Seine R.

Marne R.

PARIS

Versailles

Strasbourg

BRITTANY

Thann

Quimper

Loire R.

Tours

BURGUNDY

ATLANTIC OCEAN

SWITZERLAND

Lyon

Mont Blanc

ITALY

Bay of Biscay

Bordeaux

Nice

MONACO

Toulouse

Saintes-Maries-de-la-Mer

Marseille

French Riviera

Pyrénées Mountains

CORSICA (France)

SPAIN

ANDORRA

MEDITERRANEAN SEA

FRANCE

✳ The Louvre is France's national museum and art gallery.

What Are the Festivals?

SPRING

* **May Day**—A common tradition in France is to present loved ones with lilies, which are symbols of spring. It's also a day to celebrate the rights of workers.
* **The Gypsy Festival**—A time for gypsies to gather and honor Sarah, their patron saint, in return for good luck and blessings.
* **St. Joan of Arc Day**—On this day, people remember the great female warrior who fought for the French cause.
* **St. Bernard of Montjoux**—Honors the patron saint of mountain climbers, who is believed to make the Alpine passes safe for travelers.

SUMMER

* **Sailors' Day**—Boats are decorated with paper flowers and blessed by a priest. Children parade through the streets to the church with handmade models of ships.
* **Bastille Day**—The national day of France, which also recalls the country's road to independence.
* **Procession of the Bottles**—People walk through the town of Boulbon carrying bottles of new wine. All the people uncork their bottles at the same time and have a taste of wine.
* **Corpus Christi**—Christians eat bread and wine on this day in remembrance of Jesus Christ.
* **St. John's Day**—People light bonfires and set barrels on fire before rolling them down hills.
* **Burning of the Three Firs**—People in Thann burn three fir trees in memory of the founding of the town.
* **Tour de France**—During this popular competition, teams of ten cyclists race daily for three weeks, circling the country.
* **Cornouaille Festival**—Celebrates the Breton culture, unique to the French region of Brittany.

Don't we look nice in our special outfits? We're dressed up just for the Cornouaille Festival!

AUTUMN

* **Day of the Flutes**—Musicians parade through the streets playing ancient instruments.

* **St. Crispin's Day**—People go to church to honor the patron saint of shoes.

* **La Quintane**—Thirty men carry a box painted like a prison to the church where it is blessed. Later they smash the box.

* **Grape Harvest Festivals**—A period of celebration to mark the end of the grape-growing season.

* **St. Catherine's Day**—Unmarried women over twenty-five receive a special dinner and wear fancy hats during a parade devoted to them.

Pick up a flag and march to the sea. It's time to party in Cannes!

WINTER

* **St. Nicholas Day**—St. Nicholas, who is similar to Santa Claus, brings gifts to children who have been good throughout the year.

* **Christmas Eve**—French families gather for a traditional supper after midnight mass.

* **Christmas**—A religious holiday that commemorates the birth of Jesus Christ.

* **Epiphany**—Cakes are baked with coins inside them. Whoever gets the piece of cake with the coin is king or queen for the day.

* **New Year's Day**—The first day of the calendar year.

* **St. Bernadette of Lourdes**—Pilgrims pay homage to this saint, who was born in Lourdes, France.

* **Carnaval**—The French version of Mardi Gras, complete with masks, costumes, floats, and lots of parties.

Cornouaille Festival

For seventy years, the people of Brittany have been celebrating the Cornouaille Festival. Between the third and fourth Sundays in July, the town of Quimper in the district of Cornouaille becomes the capital of Breton culture.

A Time to Remember

Over the seven days of the festival, there are hundreds of shows, musicians, and dancers, as well as puppet shows, and traditional Breton games. The people of Brittany have good reason for holding the festival every year—to preserve their heritage and to remember their roots. For young people, Bretons, and non-Bretons alike, the Cornouaille Festival offers a chance to learn about Celtic music, history, food, and dance. People come from far and wide to see the shows and to relive history.

✳ These children are dressed in traditional Breton costumes and are ready for the Cornouaille Festival.

Where's Brittany?

Brittany is a region in northwestern France. It is the home of tiny fishing villages and huge seaports. The people of Brittany are called Bretons. Many of them still speak a form of an ancient language called Celtic, which was handed down by the original settlers of France, the Celts. There are some Bretons who are so proud of their heritage they think the best way to preserve their culture is to separate from the rest of France.

❋ Bretons perform colorful Celtic dances as part of the festivities.

Who Were the Celts?

The Celts were people who once lived throughout Europe. They settled in France about 2,500 years ago. They were bound by language, art, and a deep respect for nature. The Celts were also fierce warriors who drove chariots and fought in many battles. There are many similarities between Breton culture and that of other Celtic nations, such as Ireland and Scotland.

Breton Dress

Brittany is famous for lace making, and Breton dress is an excellent way for lace makers to show off their skills.

Breton women wear embroidered bodices, or the top part of a dress, and full skirts reaching to the floor. They also wear a **coiffe** [kwaff], a special hat made of lace. The lace is attached to a base so that it stands straight up. The coiffe can measure up to 18 inches (45 centimeters) high! In the past, people could tell which region a woman came from by the hat she wore. Her clothing also indicated if she was single or married.

Men wear baggy trousers called **bragon bas** [bra-gon bah]. They are worn to the knee and are usually made of cotton. Their vests or waistcoats are embroidered. The outfit is completed with a wide-brimmed hat and **sabots** [sa-BOW], special clogs worn on their feet.

The Parade

On the first Sunday of the Cornouaille Festival, the town organizes a huge parade. Townspeople and visitors take part to show off their beautiful costumes. The parade is led by more than five hundred musicians playing bagpipes, trumpets, and drums. The procession winds through the cobbled streets of Quimper in a blur of black clothing and white lace.

✳ The procession through Quimper is a display of the beautiful costumes worn by Bretons.

✳ Bagpipes were originally made from sheepskins and goatskins. Today they are mostly made of cloth.

THINK ABOUT THIS

The legends of King Arthur and Merlin are some of the best-loved stories in France. Arthur's father, Uther Pendragon, was the king of Brittany. His mother, Ygerne, was the duchess of Cornouaille.

Bastille Day

July 14 is a special day in France. Not only does it commemorate a very important date in French history, it is also France's national day. Millions of people stream into Paris during the month of July just to take part in the festivities. Come along and explore the importance of Bastille Day and how it is celebrated in France.

✳ The air show is one of the highlights of Bastille Day.

Why Is It Called Bastille Day?

The Bastille was a royal castle built in the fourteenth century. It was later converted into a prison. On July 14, 1789, Parisians stormed the prison. They freed the prisoners and took the building apart stone by stone. For the French people, the Bastille was a symbol of their **oppression** by the king and queen. The storming of the Bastille marked the beginning of the French Revolution, a struggle that helped the people gain their independence and establish a popular government.

✳ Left: A monument now stands in Paris on the site of the Bastille. On Bastille Day, it is decorated with French flags.

✳ Opposite: Colorful fireworks explode over the Eiffel Tower.

Bastille Day Celebrations

The festivities to honor Bastille Day start early in the morning. The daylight hours are reserved for military parades and brass bands. At night, buildings are brightly lit and firecrackers are set off in the street. Late at night, the official fireworks display begins. Red, white, and blue lights fill the sky in celebration of French nationalism. People cheer and wave their flags. The French flag is called *tricolore* [tree-coll-ORE], or three colors, because it is decorated with three bands of color—blue, white, and red.

People gather at the monument to the Bastille, where they listen to bands or join in the dancing that spills into the street. Each year, fire stations in Paris sponsor a huge dinner and ball. Firefighters dress in full uniform and wait on tables. They also play accordions to accompany the dancing that takes place.

✳ Elaborate military parades mark the start of the day when the French celebrate their nation.

The French Revolution

In the eighteenth century, the people of France were tired of the way King Louis XVI was running the country. The commoners were treated unfairly, and while the rich became richer, the poor could barely survive.

The storming of the Bastille was the beginning of a wave of changes that took place in France. A new constitution was written, and the Declaration of the Rights of Man and of the Citizen declared that "men are born and remain free and equal in rights." By working together, the French people had won a democratic government.

✳ King Louis XVI (above) and his wife, Marie Antoinette, were both killed by the new government after their defeat in the revolution.

Napoleon Bonaparte

Napoleon Bonaparte was a young and brilliant soldier who became the hero of the French people during the **revolution**. In 1804, he crowned himself emperor. Led by Napoleon, the French forces took over large parts of Europe. They were defeated by the English at the Battle of Waterloo in Belgium in 1815.

After the French defeat, the country was weak. The royal family tried to return to power, but they were defeated by the French in two more revolutions in 1830 and 1848.

✳ A young Napoleon Bonaparte.

> **THINK ABOUT THIS**
>
> The Arc de Triomphe, a famous monument in Paris, was built to celebrate the great military victories of Emperor Bonaparte. On the walls of the monument is a list of Napoleon's great victories.

Carnaval

For twelve days in February, the southern city of Nice falls under a spell. The annual Carnaval festivities transport people to a world of fantasy. The rest of France celebrates Carnaval as well, but nowhere are the decorations more elaborate and the celebrations more spirited than in Nice. The beautiful city of Nice has been celebrating Carnaval since as far back as the thirteenth century!

✳ During Carnaval, people wearing wonderful masks are a common sight all over France.

Mardi Gras

You may know the French term *Mardi Gras* [mar-dee gra] from the famous carnival that takes place in New Orleans every year. Mardi Gras means Fat Tuesday, which is another name for Shrove Tuesday. It is the day before Ash Wednesday, also the first day of Lent.

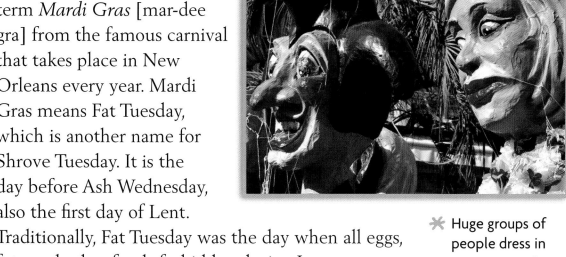

Traditionally, Fat Tuesday was the day when all eggs, fats, and other foods forbidden during Lent were eaten. It was also the day people confessed their sins. The name Shrove Tuesday comes from the old word *shrive*, which means forgiveness. Christians hope to be forgiven for all their sins on this day.

✳ Huge groups of people dress in costumes with papier-mâché masks. They are known as the "big heads."

CARNAVAL de NICE 2007
ARBITRE OFFICIEL

The Battle of Flowers

Flowers used to make perfume are grown in the south of France. Flowers have also been an important part of the Carnaval celebrations. During the twelve days of celebration, all the floats and many of the costumes for the parade are made from flowers and other plants.

One tradition that has become popular in Nice is battling with flowers. The first battle is between the floats. The crowd argues over which is the most beautiful. Later in the afternoon, the real battles begin. Everyone buys a huge bunch of flowers, and at the signal they throw them at one another. No one is safe, so it is best to have a good supply of flowers. When the fighting is finally over, everyone is covered in petals and stems.

How Did the Battles Begin?

Throwing flowers is an ancient tradition. In the past, flowers were thrown as part of a fertility ceremony. It is very similar to the tradition of throwing rice at a wedding to wish the bride and groom good luck.

✳ Even the Carnaval costumes are fashioned from flowers!

✳ Opposite: A lot of work goes into making the floats. This one may have taken months to create.

THINK ABOUT THIS

When French students came to study in New Orleans in the 1800s, they missed the Mardi Gras celebrations from home. They introduced Carnaval to their new country. Today the New Orleans celebrations are the biggest in the United States.

The Gypsy Festival

Each year in May, the small town of Saintes-Maries-de-la-Mer (Saint Marys of the Sea) is the site of one of the largest Gypsy gatherings in the world. The Gypsies, a group of people who traditionally wander from place to place, travel from far and wide to the coast of France to honor their patron saint, Sarah. The festival celebrates Sarah's return to the shores of the Mediterranean Sea. For two days, the festival spirit overtakes the town. The sound of Gypsy music can be heard everywhere.

The Legend of the Saints

The legend of the saints who gave their name to the town dates back to biblical times. In the Bible, Mary Salome and Mary Jacobe were the mothers of two apostles. They were forced to leave Palestine in a boat with no oars or sails. Sarah, a dark-skinned woman from Egypt, guided them to the shores of France, where they built an **oratory** and spread the word of Jesus Christ.

✳ Among the Gypsies, Sarah is known as Sarah la Kali, or Sarah the Dark One.

The Procession

The second day of the festival is dedicated to the saints. Gypsy pilgrims take the statue of Sarah from her **crypt** and parade her through the streets of the town in a procession. The statue is accompanied by the chorus of the crowd crying, "Long live Saint Sarah! Long live the Gypsies!" Eventually, the procession reaches its destination, the beach, and everyone makes a dash for the water. Gypsies and townspeople come together to ask for a blessing from God. The statue is then loaded on a boat and taken out to sea for a final blessing.

The statues of Saint Mary Salome and Saint Mary Jacobe are honored in the same way.

✳ The local townspeople take part in the procession as well.

The Gypsy Capital

For two days, the southern town of Saintes-Maries-de-la-Mer becomes the capital of the Gypsies. Over the years, the festival has drawn some very famous Gypsy entertainers. When the music starts, people start moving and clapping their hands. Soon everyone is singing and dancing in time with the music.

The festival is also a popular time for weddings and baptisms, which are postponed all year so they can be blessed by Saint Sarah.

The Wild South

Once the Gypsies have finished celebrating, they are eager to get back on the road. However, for some people the celebrations continue the next day with a rodeo. Saintes-Maries-de-la-Mer is in an area of France known as the Camargue. The Camargue is known as the Wild West of France, where cowboys and horses are a common sight. For the remainder of the week, people living in Camargue hold horse shows and bullfights.

✳ The locals take to the streets wearing traditional regional dress.

✳ Opposite: Bullfights and horse shows are two of the main attractions in Camargue.

> **THINK ABOUT THIS**
> Gypsies originally came from northern India, but now they can be found worldwide. They are known as travelers who move from one place to the next according to the seasons. In many countries, Gypsies are considered the guardians of tradition.

Grape Harvest Festivals

France is famous throughout the world for its wines. Every autumn, in the wine-producing areas of France, the local people celebrate the end of the grape harvest. The French call the harvest *la vendange* [la vahn-DAWN-juh]. They hold dances and taste the new wine for the first time. Members of wine societies dress in traditional robes to test the grapes and wines. Farmers and townspeople celebrate their new wines and the end of the grape-growing season.

✳ This group is tasting wine made from the newly harvested grapes.

✳ Most people in France drink wine. In some families, children are allowed to have a taste of wine on special occasions.

A Barrel of Laughs

One of the biggest harvest festivals takes place in the region of Burgundy, where three great wine-producing areas host Les Trois Glorieuses. This refers to the three glorious days in November when French people from all over the country indulge in wine tasting and folk dancing. It is also the country's most important wine auction.

Citizens of Verdigny celebrate the Festival of the New Grapes with much ceremony. Wine tasters in proper ceremonial dress sip the wine slowly before making judgments on its flavor and quality.

Even long after the harvesting season is over, the French continue to celebrate by honoring the patron saint of wine, Saint Vincent. His day falls on January 22. It is celebrated mostly by people in the villages that have vineyards.

✳ A lot of French wine is kept in oak barrels, which adds to its flavor and aroma.

Things for You to Do

France is home to some of the greatest art and artists of all time. The French have produced masterpieces of art, film, literature, and music. It is no wonder that millions of people travel to France each year to participate in the country's cultural festivals.

Paul Cézanne (1839–1906)

One of France's most famous painters is Paul Cézanne. Today Cézanne is often called the father of modern painting, but in his own time he was often criticized and misunderstood. He thought that it was important to capture the effects of light and to express his emotions in his work. Although it may seem strange now, this was a new concept in art at the time. His ideas influenced other young artists who began a **movement** in the style of Cézanne.

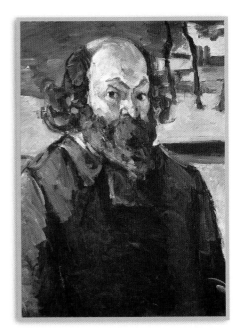

✳ A self-portrait of Paul Cézanne.

Two of Cézanne's paintings are illustrated on these pages. Look carefully at the colors he used. What kind of feelings do they bring out in you? Do they make you feel good or bad? What do you think the artist was thinking when he painted the artworks? These are all questions you can ask yourself to learn more about art.

Paint a Picture

Now try painting a picture yourself. Think of something or someone important in your life. It could be a favorite object, your friend, or a family member. It could even be you. You'll need some paints and some paper. If you're doing a self-portrait, you'll also need a mirror.

✳ This kind of painting is called a **still life**.

FURTHER INFORMATION

Books: *Find Out About France: Learn French Words and Phrases and About Life in France.* Duncan Crosbie (Barron's Educational Series, 2006).

France (Enchantment of the World. Second Series). Don Nardo (Children's Press, 2007).

Marie Antoinette, Queen of France. Mary Englar (Capstone Press, 2008).

A Visit to France. Rob Alcraft (Heinemann Library, 2008).

Websites: www.francekeys.com/english/—An informative guide that provides a snapshot of the many regions in France.

www.oxfam.org.uk/coolplanet/ontheline/explore/journey/france/frindex. htm—Embark on a virtual journey through France and find out more about French people and their way of life.

Make a Fish Mobile

April Fools' Day is known as *Poisson D'Avril* in France, or April Fish. It is one of the most popular festivals for children. It is a time to play tricks on people, tell outrageous stories, and stick cutouts of fish on people's backs. In honor of the April Fish, here's a craft activity to make a fish mobile.

You will need:
1. Cardboard
2. String
3. Scissors
4. A hole punch
5. Paints
6. Paintbrushes
7. A paint tray
8. A pencil

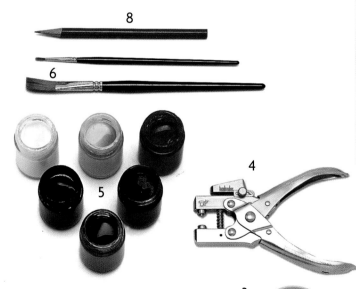

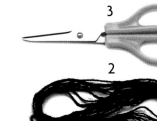

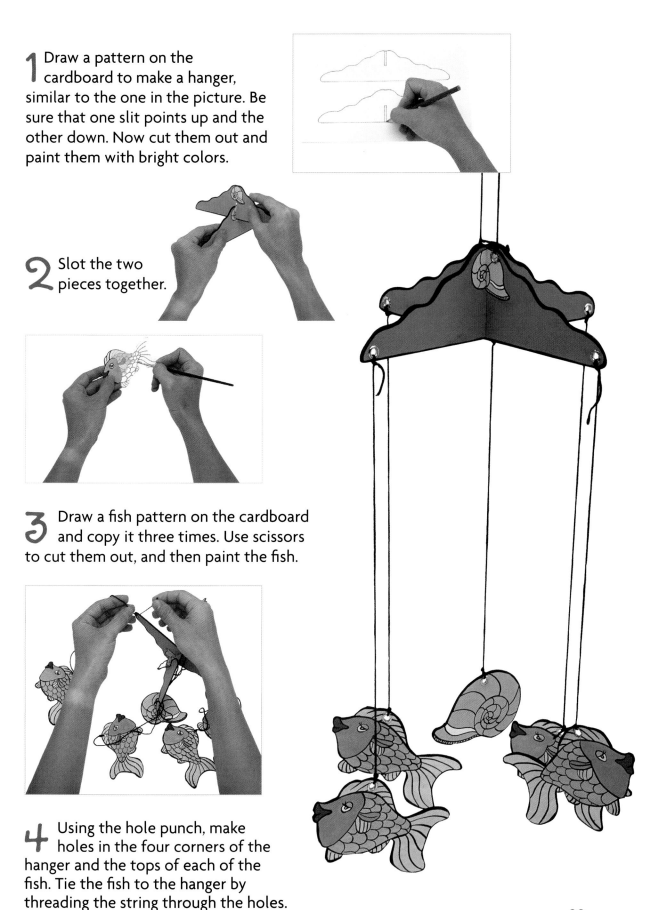

1 Draw a pattern on the cardboard to make a hanger, similar to the one in the picture. Be sure that one slit points up and the other down. Now cut them out and paint them with bright colors.

2 Slot the two pieces together.

3 Draw a fish pattern on the cardboard and copy it three times. Use scissors to cut them out, and then paint the fish.

4 Using the hole punch, make holes in the four corners of the hanger and the tops of each of the fish. Tie the fish to the hanger by threading the string through the holes.

Make a Bûche de Noël

B*ûche de Noël* means Yule log or Christmas log. It is made with chocolate cake and ice cream and makes a delicious Christmas treat. Here's the recipe so you can make your own Christmas surprise.

You will need:

1. 1/2 box chocolate cake mix
2. 1 quart (1 liter) vanilla ice cream
3. 1 egg
4. 1/2 cup (120 ml) milk
5. Chocolate frosting
6. A mixing bowl
7. A baking tray or pan
8. A wooden spoon
9. A butter knife
10. A spoon
11. A measuring cup
12. A cutting board
13. A pot holder

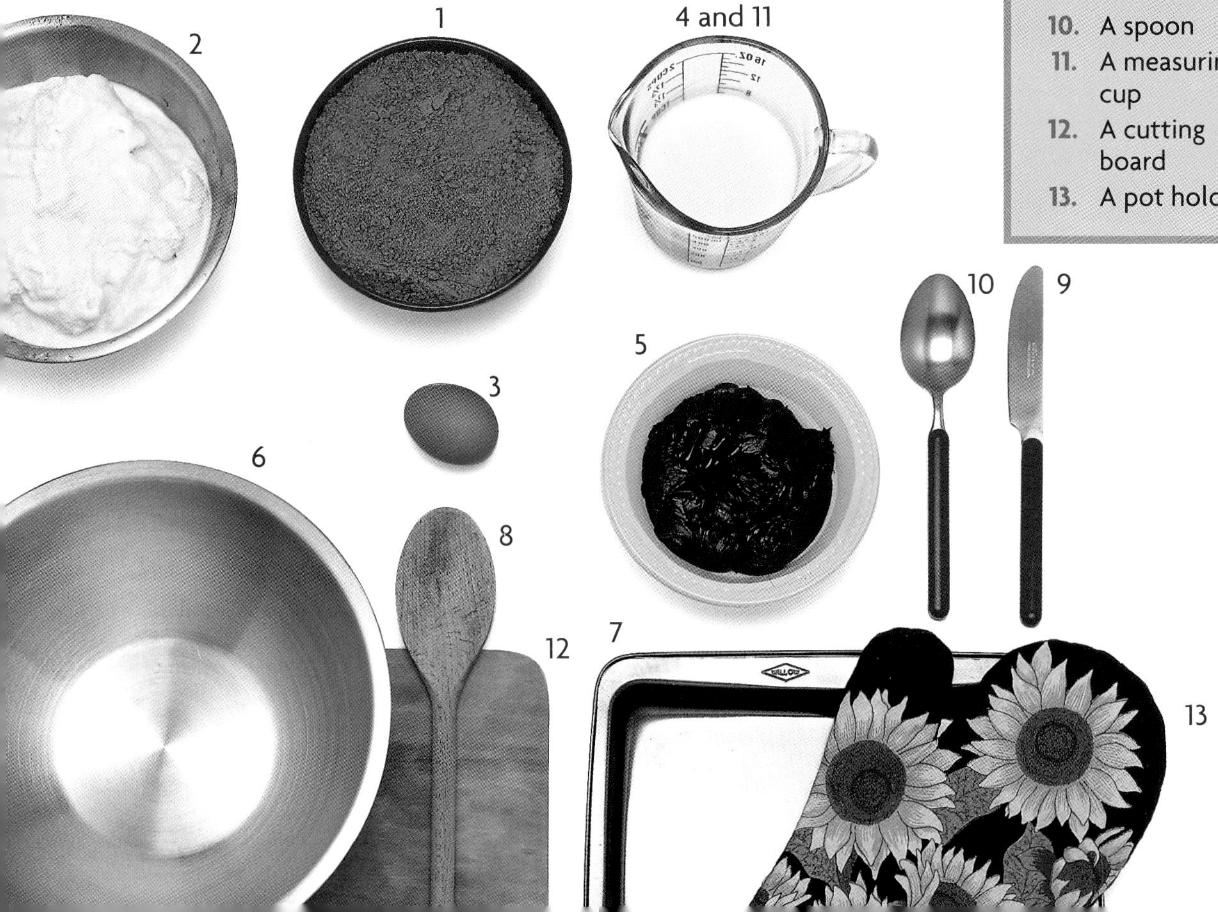
2
1
4 and 11
10
9
5
3
6
8
12
7
13

1 With clean hands, mix the egg and milk with the cake mix, or follow the instructions on the back of the box of cake mix.

2 Pour the mixture into a baking tray. With an adult's help, cook the cake according to the instructions on the box.

3 Let the cake cool, then spread the ice cream evenly over the cake.

4 Carefully roll the cake.

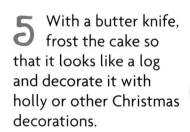

5 With a butter knife, frost the cake so that it looks like a log and decorate it with holly or other Christmas decorations.

Glossary

baguettes	Long, thin loaves of crusty bread.
bragon bas	Baggy trousers worn by Breton men.
Celts	A group of people that settled in France. The ancestors of the Bretons.
coiffe	A tall, lace hat worn by Breton women.
crypt	An underground room used as a burial place.
la vendange	The grape harvest.
movement	A group of people who work to achieve a particular goal.
oppression	To be treated unfairly or cruelly.
oratory	A room or building where people go to pray.
revolution	A successful attempt by a large group of people to change the political system of their country.
sabots	Clogs worn by Breton men.
still life	A painting or drawing of arranged objects.
tricolore	The French flag.

Index